UPSIDE DOWN LIVING
BIBLE STUDY

UPSIDE DOWN LIVING

BIBLE STUDY

A STUDY FROM THE BOOK OF ACTS

GREG LAURIE

Discipleship Inside Out®

NavPress is the publishing ministry of The Navigators, an international Christian organization and leader in personal spiritual development. NavPress is committed to helping people grow spiritually and enjoy lives of meaning and hope through personal and group resources that are biblically rooted, culturally relevant, and highly practical.

**For a free catalog go to www.NavPress.com
or call 1.800.366.7788 in the United States or 1.800.839.4769 in Canada.**

© 2012 by The Navigators

Adapted from Upside Down Living © 2009 by Greg Laurie. Used by permission of Kerygma, Inc. www.AllenDavidBooks.com

All rights reserved. No part of this publication may be reproduced in any form without written permission from NavPress, P.O. Box 35001, Colorado Springs, CO 80935. www.navpress.com

NAVPRESS and the NAVPRESS logo are registered trademarks of NavPress. Absence of ® in connection with marks of NavPress or other parties does not indicate an absence of registration of those marks.

ISBN-13: 978-1-61291-288-2

Written by Karen Lee-Thorp

Some of the anecdotal illustrations in this book are true to life and are included with the permission of the persons involved. All other illustrations are composites of real situations, and any resemblance to people living or dead is coincidental.

Unless otherwise identified, all Scripture quotations in this publication are taken from the New King James Version (NKJV). Copyright © 1982 by Thomas Nelson, Inc. Used by permission. All rights reserved. Also used is The Holy Bible, English Standard Version (ESV), copyright © 2001 by Crossway Bibles, a division of Good News Publishers. Used by permission. All rights reserved.

Printed in the United States of America

1 2 3 4 5 6 7 8 / 17 16 15 14 13 12

UPSIDE DOWN LIVING BIBLE STUDY

CONTENTS

Getting Started   7

1. Power to Change the World   11
   Acts 1:1–2:41

2. Secrets of the Early Church   21
   Acts 2:42–4:31

3. A Person God Uses   29
   Acts 4:32–8:40

4. The Last Person You'd Expect   37
   Acts 7:58–8:3; 9:1-31; 11:19-30

5. Beyond the Comfort Zone   43
   Acts 10:1–11:18; 12:1–14:28

6. Songs in the Dark   49
   Acts 16:6-40; 17:16-34

7. Making Each Day Count   55
   Acts 20:13–23:22

8. Trials and Storms   63
   Acts 23:23–27:44

Leader's Notes   71

UPSIDE DOWN LIVING BIBLE STUDY

GETTING STARTED

Notes and Observations

We often look at the book of Acts and ask, "Why can't the church today be more like that?" That's a good question! Some things are up to the Holy Spirit to do when and how He chooses, but many qualities of that first generation of believers are ours for the taking. Do you want to be part of what God is doing in the world? Acts offers you a role in that unfolding story.

Acts tells how God carried on His work in the world after Jesus rose from the dead and returned to His Father. It tells of the Holy Spirit working through great leaders and ordinary believers. At one point, missionaries named Paul and Silas were talking about Jesus in a town in what is now Greece, and a furious mob complained to the officials of the town, "These who have turned the world upside down have come here too" (Acts 17:6).

What they meant was, "These troublemakers are disturbing the peace." It was not a compliment. But for Paul and Silas it was high praise — turning the world upside down with the gospel of Jesus was exactly what they wanted to do.

British evangelist G. Campbell Morgan said, "Organized Christianity that fails to make a disturbance is dead." *Upside Down Living* looks at the way that first generation of Christians lived in order to find out how they did make a disturbance. How did they change the world? What can we learn from them that will help us accomplish God's purposes in our world?

This Bible study offers you a chance to study Acts and *Upside Down Living* on your own or with a group of friends. At the beginning of each study session you'll see which portions of Acts to read before your group meets, and which chapters of

Notes and Observations

Upside Down Living you should read. However, this study is designed to work even if you don't have time to read the book. As long as you have a Bible, you'll be fine. (You will, however, get more out of it if you read *Upside Down Living* as you go along.)

Using This Study on Your Own

Ideally you'll read the chapters of *Upside Down Living* as you read through Acts. When you've finished the week's reading, dig into the questions. Don't feel you must hurry to put down answers for all the questions. If God is talking to you through one question, stay there and pray about it or write all that comes to you. This isn't a task to complete; it's a chance for you and God to talk about your life. If you skip some questions but you've been with God, that's what matters.

If you don't have time to read the book, do read the portions of Acts. And again, quality time with God, not quantity of material covered, is what counts.

Using This Study with a Group

Again, ideally you'll read the relevant portions of *Upside Down Living* and Acts before each meeting. Even better, spend some time thinking about answers to the questions before you meet. Better still, write your answers before the group meets. Then when you meet, don't just share what you've written — discuss it. Questions and different views are okay. You can certainly have a productive discussion without prior preparation, but you'll get much more out of the study if you make time for at least the reading beforehand.

Do establish a discussion leader. This person's job is to keep the conversation moving and decide when to move to the next question. He or she doesn't need to have the answers. If you are chosen for this role, see the Leader's Notes at the end of this guide. There are tips for guiding a discussion as well as ideas for individual questions.

Sometimes you may find it helpful to have someone read the text aloud between questions. That text includes excerpts from *Upside Down Living* that help frame the questions.

Likewise, there are times when you'll want to read aloud a relevant portion of Acts. You don't need to read aloud the entire portion of Acts assigned for each session if most of the group is reading it at home. But if people aren't reading it at home, read it in the group. Acts is full of exciting stories that are quick to read. You may even enjoy reading some of the stories like a play, assigning different characters' parts to different readers. There are instructions for doing this in the Leader's Notes.

Finally, be as honest as you can with the members of your group. Having other people in your life who know what's going on with you and are supporting you, praying for you, and challenging your thinking will benefit you and help you grow spiritually.

Notes and Observations

ONE
POWER TO CHANGE THE WORLD
Acts 1:1–2:41

> **To prepare for this discussion, please read:**
> - Acts 1:1–2:41
> - Chapters 1 and 2 of *Upside Down Living*

We have bills to pay. We have jobs, families, responsibilities at church, demanding course loads at school. As busy as we are, we may come to the book of Acts with a mix of guilt, frustration, and longing: "You want me to be part of changing the world the way the first generation of Christians did? I barely have time to change the oil in my car. But yeah, I wish I could be part of that. I'd like to look back on my life someday and know that it was about something."

Being part of what God is doing in the world is not cost-free — Acts makes that clear. What each of us needs to decide is, is it worth it? Peter, Paul, and the rest of the early Christians we'll be talking about surely thought so. But before we jump to that question, we need answers to two others:

a. What part does God want us to have in changing the world?
b. How is it possible, given our obvious limitations?

Acts 1:1–2:41 points us toward answers to these questions.

Notes and Observations

1. In terms of your natural temperament, where would you put yourself on a scale of boldness in relationships with other people?

1	2	3	4	5	6	7	8	9	10
very shy									very bold

2. In a situation where someone has to proclaim the gospel to nonbelievers, which of these roles would you most likely take on?
   a. I'd be Peter preaching boldly to the crowd.
   b. I'd be praying for the Holy Spirit to speak through Peter, or praying for the crowd.
   c. I'd go and talk one-on-one with someone I recognized in the crowd.
   d. I'd slip out the back door.
   e. Other (describe it):

And He said to them, "It is not for you to know times or seasons which the Father has put in His own authority. But you shall receive power when the Holy Spirit has come upon you; and you shall be witnesses to Me in Jerusalem, and in all Judea and Samaria, and to the end of the earth." (1:7-8)

The words above were the last words Jesus spoke before His ascension....

    The apostles were in no way ready for such a task. There was still much they didn't understand. Their faith was weak. They had failed in their public witness and also in their private faith. Even Simon Peter, their acknowledged leader, had openly denied the Lord. If *Peter* could be intimidated and demoralized by the words of a servant girl in the high priest's courtyard, how could any of them be expected to go anywhere and preach anything?

Jesus answered that question, too.

How would they do it? They would do it with a power they had never known before. A power beyond anything they had yet experienced. A power to change the world. (*Upside Down Living* 22–23)

3. In an ordinary, nonreligious sense, what is a witness? What does a witness do?

4. What do you think Jesus meant when He told His disciples, "You shall be witnesses to Me" (Acts 1:8)?

5. What are some other ways of being a witness to Jesus besides speaking in front of large groups?

When it comes to being witnesses about what we know of Jesus Christ, we're not dependent on our natural temperaments. The power to be Jesus' witnesses comes from the Holy Spirit (1:8). Sure enough, that's what happens in Acts 2.

One way we could translate the Greek term of being "filled with the Spirit" is with the picture of wind filling a sail. So in Ephesians 5:18, when Paul says, "Be filled with the Spirit," he is essentially saying, "May the wind of the Spirit fill your sail and guide your course through life."

Notes and Observations

Notes and Observations

Have you ever been out in a sailboat and found yourself with no wind? It's a lot of work to row back to shore! And then a gust of wind comes along, you quickly hoist your sail, and find yourself cruising across the waves again. And you say to yourself, "Ahh . . . now this is the way it ought to be."

That's a pretty good picture of what it's like in the Christian life when we try to do what God has told us to do in our strength. It's like rowing a sailboat! You know, we grit our teeth, and really dig in, saying, "I've got to obey the Lord, and keep my thoughts pure, and witness to my neighbors, and love my spouse, and resist temptation. . . ." And it's hard going! We find ourselves with blisters on our blisters.

But then we come to our senses, and say, "Lord, I can't row this boat on my own. I ask that Your Holy Spirit will fill my sail and help me accomplish what I can't accomplish in my own strength."

When we do that, what has seemed like duty to us begins to feel more like delight.

To be filled with the Holy Spirit means that I am carried along by and under the control of Jesus Christ. I fill my mind and heart with His Word so that His thoughts become my thoughts. To be filled with the Holy Spirit is to walk thought-by-thought, decision-by-decision, act-by-act, under the Spirit's control. (*Upside Down Living* 32)

6. How would you explain being filled with the Holy Spirit to someone who isn't familiar with the idea? Is the above explanation helpful to you? If so, in what ways?

7. What investment of time would it take (or does it take) to fill your mind and heart with God's Word to the point where His thoughts become your thoughts?

What are the challenges of doing that in your present life situation?

How are you dealing with those challenges? Or how could you deal with them? What help, if any, do you need?

Before you are a Christian, the Holy Spirit is *with you*. In other words, He is working in your life to convince you that you need Jesus Christ and His saving work in your life. Then, once you receive Christ into your life, the Holy Spirit comes and lives *inside of you*. The Bible teaches that the Holy Spirit indwells every Christian. As believers we are sealed and led by the Holy Spirit.

In Acts 1:8, however, Jesus speaks of something more than the Spirit coming to indwell you. He speaks of the empowerment you will receive when the Holy Spirit *comes upon you*. . . .

What kind of power? Not political power. We see the struggle for political power every night on the news. It seems like people will say or do almost anything to obtain such power. That's not the power Jesus speaks of here. It's not the power to overthrow Rome, or any other government. Jesus says, "No. I am offering you dynamic *spiritual*

Notes and Observations

power. Power to preach the gospel. Power to change the world. Power that will come upon you."

If you are a Christian, the Holy Spirit already lives inside of you. *But has He come upon you?* Have you ever said something like this? "Lord, empower me with Your Holy Spirit to bring the gospel to my sphere of influence." (*Upside Down Living* 24–25)

8. Have you ever prayed something like, "Lord, empower me with Your Holy Spirit to bring the gospel to my sphere of influence"? If so, what have been the results? If not, what's your honest reaction to the idea of praying this persistently? For instance, is this something you truly desire?

One of the challenges we face today as we seek to spread the gospel is scaling the language barrier. We can no longer assume that our hearers or listeners know what we're talking about. (*Upside Down Living* 37)

9. Think of someone you know who has no Christian background. How could you talk about the following concepts in words this person would understand? (The passages in parentheses may spark your thinking, but try to use words that someone who doesn't know the Bible could relate to.)

Faith (Matthew 8:5-10; John 1:12; Hebrews 11:1,6-19; James 2:14-23)

Notes and Observations

Sin (James 4:1-3; 1 John 2:15-17; 3:4)

Repent (Matthew 21:28-32; Luke 15:11-20)

It's not enough to tell people what they need to take hold of: Jesus. We also need to help them understand what they need to let go of: sin. Real faith involves trust in Jesus and surrender to Jesus, which includes the willingness to give up habits that He hates.

10. What are the challenges of talking about sin today?

What can we do about that? What can God do?

To effectively communicate the gospel to someone, it helps to know a little bit about him or her. And guess what? Everybody's favorite subject is himself or herself! . . . I will ask them questions, and then listen to their answers. (*Upside Down Living* 37)

Notes and Observations

11. Make a list of questions you think would be helpful to ask in a conversation with someone in order to communicate the gospel effectively. (There are a few suggestions in the Leader's Notes at the end of this guide, but try to make your own list before you look there. Then build on any ideas you get from those suggestions.)

12. At the core of the gospel is the story of Jesus. If you're using this guide on your own, write down what you believe are the highlights of this story. If you're meeting with a group, divide into groups of two or three and work together to summarize the story. You can consult Peter's version in Acts 2, but take into account he was talking to Jews who (a) knew the Old Testament and (b) were in the city where Jesus had recently been crucified. Try to frame your story for people today. Afterward, give the groups a chance to share their stories.

13. When the Jerusalem community was preparing to be Jesus' witnesses, prayer was central (1:14). Take some time to pray about being Jesus' witnesses. Some things you might take to God are:

- The names of particular nonbelievers in your sphere of influence — people you encounter in your family, work, children's activities, gym, anywhere. (Consider making a list of names to pray for

throughout this study. If you're meeting with a group, you could make a shared list.)
- Your fears and questions about sharing your faith.
- Your desire for the Holy Spirit to empower you to do what God has called you to do.

Notes and Observations

TWO
SECRETS OF THE EARLY CHURCH
Acts 2:42–4:31

> To prepare for this discussion, please read:
> ▶ Acts 2:42–4:31
> ▶ Chapters 3 through 5 of *Upside Down Living*

Hurry affects us spiritually, far more than we realize. In 1973, social psychologists John M. Darley and C. Daniel Batson studied the behavior of some seminary students. They told each student he needed to cross the campus to give a sermon — on the Good Samaritan, for instance. Some of the students were told they were late and needed to hurry, some were told they were just on time, and some were told they had plenty of time. On their way across campus, each student passed a man (an actor) slumped in a doorway, coughing and groaning. Only 10 percent of the students who thought they were late stopped to help the man — even if they were hurrying to preach about the Good Samaritan. But 45 percent of those in a moderate hurry stopped, while 63 percent of those with plenty of time stopped.

It's hard to keep our priorities straight when we're rushed. If we feel we don't have time for worship or prayer or helping someone in need or building a relationship with a nonbeliever, then maybe hurry is an enemy we need to stand against. Who says we don't have time to live like the early church? Maybe that's a voice we need to talk back to.

Notes and Observations

1. Look back over the past twenty-four hours. When (if at all) were you in a hurry? How did being rushed affect the way you dealt with other people? With God?

In the book of Acts, we encounter the Church that changed the world. The Church that turned the world upside down. What was their secret?

It is the simple fact that every Christian believed they were called to do his or her part. Every person mattered.

A Spartan king once boasted to a visiting monarch about the superb, impenetrable walls of Sparta. The visiting king, however, was somewhat confused by these claims; as he looked around, he could see no city walls at all. "Where are these walls you speak of?" he asked.

For a reply, the Spartan king gestured around him at his bodyguard of magnificent troops. "Just look around you," he said. "Here are the walls of Sparta. Every man is a brick."

In the same way, in the Church every man and every woman is a brick—or as the Bible terms it, *a living stone*. It's easy for someone to stand on the sidelines and be critical of the Church—pointing out all the areas where it's falling short. But God never called us to stand on the sidelines. He called us to be involved in His Church, fighting the battles, standing toe to toe with enemies in the arena. (*Upside Down Living* 52–53)

2. Do you believe you matter to what God is doing in the world? What helps you believe that? What gets in the way?

> If you are really Spirit-filled, you will love the Word of God. If you have no interest in the Bible, if you find Scripture boring and uninteresting and don't really care about reading and studying it, I have to wonder if you've been filled with the Holy Spirit at all — or if you even know the Lord Jesus as your Savior. (*Upside Down Living* 60)

3. Which of the priorities of the early church, listed in Acts 2:42-47, are currently priorities for you? Which do you currently have trouble making space for? Why do you suppose those are challenging for you?

The apostles' teaching (individual and/or group study of God's Word)

Fellowship (serving with, caring for, and sharing meals and life with other Christians)

Sharing what one has with those in need

Notes and Observations

Communion, or the Lord's Supper

Prayer (individually and/or with others)

Praising God

4. Acts 2:43 says the early believers had "fear" of God as well as joy. They took Him seriously and didn't imagine that they (or any other humans) were in charge. How did Peter and John display fear of God in 3:1–4:20?

How does the community's prayer in 4:23-31 display the fear of God?

How does the fear of God affect their fear of other things?

5. Do you fear God? If so, how does that affect the way you deal with life?

Notes and Observations

What do you think helps us cultivate a healthy fear of God?

> Yes, praise and worship can sometimes be a sacrifice, because we don't feel like engaging in it. Our flesh resists it, it doesn't seem convenient. Or perhaps we feel a bit down and depressed, and things aren't going well for us. Maybe you've experienced a real tragedy in your life, and just don't want to thank God.
>
> Worship is not about you, it's about God. It's not about how you feel in any given moment, it's about the worthiness of the One we honor. . . .
>
> There is a direct connection between worship and witness. We *are* being watched by the outside world. And when a Christian can praise God through his or her tears, when a believer can hold high the name of the Lord even in a time of hardship or tragedy, it is a powerful testimony to those who observe. (*Upside Down Living* 72, 74)

6. What could lead us to believe that worship is about us?

Notes and Observations

7. What does it mean to praise God through your tears? Are we supposed to fake it? Keep up a relentless stream of happy talk?

When the believers in Jerusalem parted company on Sunday, they didn't say, "See you next Sunday."

What they shared together wasn't just a Sunday-morning-go-to-meeting kind of Christianity. It was their very lives, and they met all the time. Something was always going on. They had home Bible studies. They had meals together. In fact, they "*shared their meals with great joy and generosity. . . .*"

In other words, they ate together often with plenty for all, and there was lots of laughter.

I love that. I love that the Bible's template for the Church included *eating*. At some point, they began to be called "love feasts." Like a modern potluck—or, in some parts of the country, a "covered dish supper"—people would bring food to eat and food to share. For some who were impoverished, this might be the one good meal you would get in a day.

So the believers would gather in different homes, break bread together, have some laughter and fun, maybe do a little singing, and talk about the things of God with one another. Then, before everyone went home, they would often end with communion, or "the Lord's supper," where they would receive the broken bread and the cup, and remember their Lord's broken body and shed blood. (*Upside Down Living* 76–77)

8. What is one quality the people of the early church had (as depicted in 2:42–4:31) that you believe God wants you to have more of?

9. Sometimes we cultivate a quality by just doing something — do what God says. At other times, it's more a matter of doing less of something else, or praying about something, or making space to contemplate who God is. What do you think God would have you do in response to what you've been studying?

10. Read aloud the prayer in Acts 4:24-30. Then write or speak your own prayer modeled on that one. If you're meeting with a group, you can divide into groups of two or three for this prayer. Pray for your partner(s) for boldness and whatever else they need. Pray for the nonbelievers in your lives, even those who are hostile to the gospel.

UPSIDE DOWN LIVING BIBLE STUDY

Notes and Observations

THREE
A PERSON GOD USES
Acts 4:32–8:40

> To prepare for this discussion, please read:
>
> ▶ Acts 4:32–8:40
> ▶ Chapters 6 through 8 of *Upside Down Living*

Our society is obsessed with image. Celebrities pay publicists to manage what people think of them, stylists to buy clothes that will project their desired image, as well as hair and makeup artists, personal trainers, and social networking consultants. Then paparazzi pursue them in hopes of catching them in an unguarded moment that will reveal their "real" selves. Politicians, too, need legions of staff to tell them how to spin a story and how to appear to be what the public wants.

This sort of behavior is everywhere today, but it's nothing new. The first generation of Christians faced the same challenge: Will I be courageous and pay the price when people don't like hearing the truth, or will it be enough to *appear* courageous? If I'm not as repentant, worshipful, generous, loving, and evangelistic as someone else, can I fake it? In Acts 4:32–8:40 we meet some people who opt for faking it and some who are the real thing.

Notes and Observations

1. What is one part of your life where it seems to matter (to you or to someone else) what people think of you?

2. In Acts 5:1-8, what do Ananias and Sapphira want people to believe about them?

> At this point, the young church was living together communally. Because of the persecution in those days, believers had lost their homes and their jobs, so other believers who had resources and means were helping out. Everybody had the option of doing whatever the Lord led them to do. Some were taking properties, selling them, and giving the money to the Church, but not everyone was doing that. It was up to the individual before God.
>
> It was a very unique and precious time in the life of the infant church, and the world looked on in amazement as these believers poured out their lives for one another. (*Upside Down Living* 108)

3. Why does Peter refer to Ananias and Sapphira's behavior as lying to the Holy Spirit? Why isn't it just lying to the church?

> A hypocrite is *not* someone who believes something, and then falls short of that belief. If that were true, we'd all have to wear that label. All of us fall short of our beliefs and ideals at one time or another. We have standards that we seek to live by, and we fail to meet those marks time after time.

> But as I said, that doesn't make us hypocrites, that makes us *human*. We are imperfect people trying to serve a perfect God....
>
> A hypocrite is something different altogether. The word *hypocrite* comes from a Greek term that means "to wear a mask." Paul's readers would have been familiar with Greek theater, where all the actors wore masks. A hypocrite, then, is an actor—someone pretending to be someone or something they're not. (*Upside Down Living* 100–101)

4. In session 2 we saw that sometimes it's necessary to praise God even when we don't feel like it. How is that different from hypocrisy?

5. Under what circumstances might it be hypocritical to sing worship songs to God?

From the negative examples of Ananias and Sapphira, we move to the positive examples of Stephen and Philip:

> Our objective as Christians shouldn't be a long life as much as a full and meaningful one. A life with purpose....
>
> As we look at Stephen's life we see a life that is well lived. And we also discover the kind of man or woman God is looking for to use for His glory. (*Upside Down Living* 115)

6. What does Stephen say and do in Acts 6–7 that demonstrates a life well lived?

Notes and Observations

Knowing the Bible as he did made [Stephen] a powerful instrument in the Lord's hands, but it was his God-given wisdom that instructed him on how to use and apply that knowledge. Here's the sad truth: You can have a vast amount of knowledge—even Bible knowledge—but if you aren't guided by the Holy Spirit and godly wisdom, that learning will be of little help to you or those in your life. (*Upside Down Living* 120)

7. How would you define each of Stephen's qualities in your own words? Give a practical example of what each one looks like in action:

Full of the Holy Spirit (Acts 6:3; *Upside Down Living* 120)

Wisdom (Acts 6:3; *Upside Down Living* 120)

Faithfulness (*Upside Down Living* 120–122)

8. What do you think the text means when it says that Stephen's face was like the face of an angel (6:15)? How does an angel's face look?

Why did Stephen's face look like that?

Notes and Observations

> "Well Greg," you say, "I wish I felt the joy of the Lord in my life. I feel like I've become dried up, spiritually."
>
> Let me ask you this: How long has it been since you've shared your faith with someone? The Christian life isn't meant to be hoarded, it's meant to be shared. We're told in Proverbs 11:25, "The one who blesses others is abundantly blessed; those who help others are helped."
>
> You have been blessed to be a blessing to others. . . .
>
> As you start declaring what God has done for you, *it will become more real for you as you make it real to them.* . . .
>
> If you begin ministering in the name of Jesus and in the power of the Holy Spirit, if you begin helping someone who is hurting even worse than you, you too will be changed by the power of God. (*Upside Down Living* 124–126)

9. Have you ever experienced strengthened faith or encouragement after ministering to someone else? If so, describe what happened.

10. Stephen told people the truth about Jesus, and when he was attacked, he responded not with self-pity or condemnation, but with forgiveness (7:59-60). How do you typically respond when you are personally attacked, or when you hear through the media about attacks on Christians?

Notes and Observations

11. What do you think it takes to become like Stephen in this regard?

After Stephen's murder, the mob that had admired Christians turned hostile, and the authorities seized the chance to try to stamp out the fledgling movement. Many Christians were driven out of Jerusalem. Philip was one of them. But the Holy Spirit employed refugees like Philip as messengers of the gospel. Instead of sticking to people like himself, Philip now took the gospel to people who were very different: Samaritans (8:4-8) and an African government official (8:26-40).

> Most of us prefer to hang around people who are most like us, don't we? We feel naturally inclined toward people who look like us, talk like us, and have the same interests as us. We're uncomfortable when we find ourselves in a group that holds different values than we do, and speaks or dresses in ways so very different from our own circle of friends and acquaintances.
> But what if God calls you to such a group or such an individual? Would you be willing to make yourself uncomfortable for His sake? (*Upside Down Living* 141)

12. In a typical week, what contact do you have with people who hold different values from yours?

13. How do you typically relate to such people?

14. How would you like to relate to such people?

Notes and Observations

When it comes to sharing vital truth about sin and salvation,

> There has to come a moment where we say to ourselves, "You know what? It's not about me. It's not about whether I feel comfortable or don't feel comfortable. It's about me obeying the Lord." (*Upside Down Living* 138)

15. No matter how bold or articulate we are, only God can enable someone to surrender to the Holy Spirit and choose faith in Jesus. Pray for the nonbelievers you named in session 1 and those whom you've been thinking about in this session. Ask God to make them aware of their need for Him. Ask Him to provide opportunities for you to talk with them, as He did for Philip with the Ethiopian official. Ask Him to give you courage like Stephen and Philip. Ask for the right words and for help in obeying Him despite your discomfort.

Tell God honestly how you feel about speaking of Him with nonbelievers. If you're meeting with a group, your group shouldn't be a place where you need to appear more loving or bold than you are. It should be a safe place for people to tell the truth about how much they feel they can give God at this time. Ask God to help you not fake it with each other.

FOUR
THE LAST PERSON YOU'D EXPECT
Acts 7:58–8:3; 9:1-31; 11:19-30

> To prepare for this discussion, please read:
> ▶ Acts 7:58–8:3; 9:1-31; 11:19-30
> ▶ Chapters 9 and 10 of *Upside Down Living*

Who in your life is the last person you'd expect to come to faith in Jesus Christ? Maybe it's the person in your office who is always needling you about your beliefs. It seems like every week she has ten new questions to fire at you. At times she seems downright hostile. She may even make fun of you in front of people because of your faith.

Or maybe it's the family member who isn't rude like that, but just tunes you out when you talk about your faith. You sense by the way he lives and by his utter lack of interest in Christian things that he's a million miles from God.

Saul of Tarsus was one of the hostile ones, hostile in ways that would be illegal today in countries with freedom of religion. And yet, to the bewilderment of those who knew about him, he changed. In this session we'll look at why and how much he changed, and at two of the key people who helped him.

Notes and Observations

1. Who is someone in your life you can't imagine will ever come to faith in Jesus Christ? What is it about that person that makes him or her seem so unlikely?

2. In Acts 7:58–8:3, how does Saul initially react to Stephen's death?

What does his reaction tell you about him?

Stephen's executioners laid their coats at Saul's feet, indicating that he was probably in charge of this bloody operation. I wonder if Stephen looked right into his eyes as he called on the Lord to forgive his murderers. I wonder if he was thinking, *"Oh Lord, if You would save a man like Saul—what a change You could bring to the world through Him!"*

Saul of Tarsus, of course, did come to faith in Jesus Christ, and became the man we now know as the apostle Paul. . . .

He would never forget that terrible day, and I believe it was a turning point in his life. A man who was driven by hate became a man motivated for the rest of his life by love, and I believe that Stephen was the one who reached him more than any other. So Stephen may not have had many converts, but he had one in the apostle Paul that would lead to the conversion of untold millions—make that, *billions*—of others. (*Upside Down Living* 129)

3. In 9:4-5, Jesus tells Saul that he has been persecuting Jesus Himself. Why Jesus Himself, not simply those who believe in Jesus?

Notes and Observations

The light from heaven blinded Saul, and after his companions helped him to Damascus he spent three days fasting and praying.

> I wonder what Saul was praying about. I have a strong hunch he was asking the Lord for forgiveness. Blind and alone in that room in Damascus, it was dawning on him what he had done. . . . He was—possibly for the first time—really seeing himself, and seeing his actions for what they were. . . .
> But I think he probably worshipped as he prayed, as well. (*Upside Down Living* 175)

4. What does it tell you about God that He forgave and called someone like Saul?

5. While Saul was talking to the Lord, the Lord was also talking to Ananias (9:11-16). What was the Lord saying?

Why didn't Ananias want to do what the Lord was telling him to do?

Notes and Observations

6. What character qualities does Ananias's response show?

> Ananias did what God said, and became part of a story that will be told and retold throughout eternity. The fact is, you do have a choice when God gives you a task: you can obey, and reap the wonderful fruits and rewards of that decision, or you can refuse and forfeit the blessing that would have been yours. How big a blessing? That's just it . . . you'll never know. (*Upside Down Living* 158)

7. Is there a task or command from God that you currently find hard to obey? What are the risks of saying yes? What are the risks of saying no?

8. Barnabas was another hero who touched Saul's life. What do we know about him from these passages:

4:36-37

9:26-28

11:19-26

9. Who has been an Ananias or a Barnabas for you — praying for you, introducing you when you were a stranger, or encouraging you to use your gifts?

> Someone, somewhere, probably right now, needs you to stand in the gap. . . . You don't have to know every Bible verse, or the answer to all those difficult theological questions. You just need to be a real Christian who can show them what it's like to live in the real world, help them acclimate, and encourage them to become a part of the Church. (*Upside Down Living* 163)

10. What goes through your mind when you think about being a role model and encourager for a young believer? (You don't have to share a name with your group, but take a moment to ask God if there's a person He has in mind for you.)

> If you face calamity, if you have a loved one die unexpectedly, if you have a physical infirmity you are struggling with, and you can still rejoice, praise God, and maintain a peaceful spirit, now that, my friend, is a powerful witness.
>
> After all, how will they find out that God's grace is sufficient for their needs, unless they first see how His grace has been sufficient for *your* needs? (*Upside Down Living* 178)

Notes and Observations

11. The Lord didn't just call Saul to be a great leader. He called him to suffer (9:16). How do you respond to the idea of God calling you to suffer as a witness of His grace?

12. If you're meeting with a group, how can the group pray for you? For you — not just for your friend or relative. Maybe God is asking you to suffer or has given you a task that seems daunting. Maybe you need to know how to be effective in a younger believer's life, or maybe you're not sure what God is asking of you.

    Pray for the nonbelievers you listed in session 1, and pray also for one another.

    If you're not meeting with a group, write down your prayer here.

FIVE
BEYOND THE COMFORT ZONE
Acts 10:1–11:18; 12:1–14:28

> **To prepare for this discussion, please read:**
> - Acts 10:1–11:18; 12:1–14:28
> - Chapters 11 through 13 of *Upside Down Living*

It's hard to overstate how uncomfortable most American Christians were with the hippie counterculture in the late 1960s. Long hair and bare feet; sex, drugs, and rock and roll — the best people hoped for was to protect their own children from being infected by the decadence. But Kay Smith had a heart for hippies, and her heart moved her husband, Chuck. Their church's outreach to hippies became a pivotal part of the revival that came to be known as the Jesus Movement.

The horror with which many Christians looked upon hippies in the 1960s was mild compared to the disgust devout Jews had for Gentiles in the time of Peter and Saul. The Gentiles worshipped false gods. God had worked for centuries to keep His people separate from pagans so that they wouldn't be assimilated into pagan culture. Entering a Gentile home made a good Jew unclean for temple worship. Gentiles ate foods that were both forbidden and revolting to Jews. The disgust was understandable, but if believers like Peter, Barnabas, and Saul had not overcome it, the church would have remained a tiny sect within Judaism. In this session we'll look at how God worked with His people to move them way

Notes and Observations

beyond their comfort zone, into the homes of outsiders and into the valley of suffering.

1. When it comes to trying new foods and experiences and traveling to unfamiliar places, which of the following best describes you?

   a. I've traveled widely, I enjoy unfamiliar cultures, and I love tasting new things that other people might think are weird.
   b. I like to travel, but not to places that are too exotic or risky. I like to try new foods, but nothing too extreme.
   c. I enjoy what's familiar and don't feel a tremendous urge to experiment.
   d. Other (describe your views on getting out of your comfort zone):

2. Peter's vision in Acts 10:9-16 challenged him to break the kosher food laws, to eat foods forbidden in the book of Leviticus. What was God communicating through this vision? How would you put verse 15 into your own words?

Is there a "Cornelius" in your life? Is there someone rubbing up against your world who makes you feel uncomfortable because he or she is so "different," or holds values that are so opposite from your own? Does the thought of reaching out to that person with the Good News about Jesus make you want to run in the opposite direction? Maybe this is an individual you would regard as an enemy, and deep down you're not even sure if you *want* them to find forgiveness in Christ and go to heaven. (*Upside Down Living* 191–192)

3. Take a moment to ask God if there is a Cornelius in your life, or a group of them. Is God asking you to reach out to some individual? If it's a group you can't imagine going to personally, could you support an organization that does reach that group?

Peter and the rest of the Jerusalem-based church were obedient to God, yet God allowed their faith to be tested again, this time through persecution. Herod executed James the brother of John and then arrested Peter (12:1-3). God rescued Peter from prison, but He didn't rescue James.

Sometimes when a crisis overwhelms us and we call out to God, He will step in and change our circumstances. . . . But there are other times when He will say, "No, My child, you must drink it. You have to go through it." . . . And if we believe in the providence of God, we know that the Lord is in control of all things, even those events that hurt and grieve us. (*Upside Down Living* 187)

4. How do you respond to a God who rescued Peter but not James, who is able to rescue us from suffering but sometimes chooses not to? Does a particular situation come to mind when you think about this?

Notes and Observations

Notes and Observations

5. What reasons do we have to trust God when we don't understand why He has allowed something?

The community's prayers for Peter had a role in his miraculous escape (12:5). Effective prayer:

- Focuses on God rather than obsessing about our needs or trying to impress others with our profound words
- Seeks to align with God's will rather than change God's mind
- Is therefore rooted in a knowledge of God's heart as expressed in God's Word
- Is passionate and persistent, not discouraged or frustrated by waiting
- Is offered in unity with others
- Isn't always perfectly free from doubt

6. Which of these aspects of effective prayer do you especially need to remember at present? Why are those aspects so significant right now?

7. When has God taken a long time to answer one of your prayers?

When has He answered not with "yes" but with "this is a chance for you to grow"?

Notes and Observations

> The essence of the Christian life is knowing God and walking with Him. It's about sticking with Him when the sky is blue and also when it's filled with clouds or choked with smoke. It's about walking with the Lord through thick and thin, and pressing on through every heartache and trial that comes our way. (*Upside Down Living* 210)

8. What qualities does Paul display in 14:19-22?

9. What would those qualities look like in your life?

10. How do you think a person gets to be that way?

11. If you're meeting with a group and some group members are going through a time of suffering, take time to pray for them. Ask God to work for good in their situation. Ask Him to give you passion and persistence in praying for them. (If you're using this Bible study on your own, make a list of people you know who are suffering, and pray for them.)

Notes and Observations

If no one in your group is significantly suffering, spend some time thanking God for the ways He's caring for each of you. Ask Him to deliver you from the pride and self-satisfaction that comfort can produce. Acknowledge your dependence on Him for things you tend to take for granted. Search your lives for things to be grateful for.

SIX
SONGS IN THE DARK
Acts 16:6-40; 17:16-34

> To prepare for this discussion, please read:
>
> ▶ Acts 16:6-40; 17:16-34
> ▶ Chapters 14 and 15 of *Upside Down Living*

Notes and Observations

One of the amazing things about the apostle Paul was his focus. Athletes speak of being "in the zone," where self-consciousness falls away and their whole being is focused on the task in the moment. Paul lived in the zone. He wasn't competing against the other apostles to see who could convert the most people. He wasn't competing against the philosophers-for-hire who traveled the Roman Empire in search of students. His Master had given him a mission, and whether he was discoursing with intellectuals or lying half dead from a beating, every moment was a chance to live the mission.

In session 1 we posed a question: Do we want to be part of changing the world as the first generation of Christians did? Is it worth it? Paul clearly thought it was worth it. In this session, as we look at both his passion and the price he paid to live it, we can ask ourselves if we agree with him.

1. On a scale of 1 to 5, how easy is it for you to praise God in your current circumstances?

1	2	3	4	5
extremely hard				extremely easy

Notes and Observations

2. What is one thing for which you can honestly praise God, regardless of your current circumstances?

Philippi wasn't originally on Paul's itinerary. It had a tiny Jewish population and many anti-Semitic citizens. Yet God specifically told Paul in a vision to share the gospel there (Acts 16:7-10). The immediate results were not remotely encouraging.

3. Describe the various hardships, both mental and physical, Paul and his companion Silas suffer in Acts 16:6-24.

Have you ever seen anyone beaten with a baton or a club? It isn't a pretty sight. Paul and Silas had to be bruised and bloodied by this point. . . .

   So after being beaten with wooden rods, they were thrown into a filthy, dark, underground hole, with their legs clamped in stocks. That means that their naked backs were in the dirt, and their legs were put in stocks, pulled as far apart as possible, causing excruciating pain. (*Upside Down Living* 233–234)

4. Why do you think Paul and Silas sing praise songs to God at midnight (16:25)? What do you think they believe about God? About their situation? About suffering? About nonbelievers?

5. What positive things came out of their efforts in Philippi?

Notes and Observations

6. What would you be willing to go through to have that kind of effect on your world? Where would you draw the line?

Not all of us would take the risks for the gospel that Paul and Silas were willing to take. But God can call us into various degrees of suffering even if we haven't gone out of our way to be missionaries.

> There is a lost world all around us, and they are both watching us and listening to us. They're watching and listening when things go well for us, and when they don't go well. And sometimes they say things like this: "Well, you Christians are so thankful to God when everything is going your way. What about when crisis hits you? What about when tragedy befalls you? How are you going to deal with it?"
>
> When they see you and I giving praise to God even in difficult circumstances, even when our hearts are breaking, it opens up a door for a ministry opportunity. And suddenly certain people will listen to what we have to say who would not have listened to us otherwise. (*Upside Down Living* 236)

7. How do you react to the idea that lost people are watching the way you live your life through the good and bad times? Do you think it's true? Does it motivate you? Does it make you feel angry or bad about yourself? Explain.

Notes and Observations

After they leave Philippi, Paul's team travels across Macedonia (what is now northern Greece) and suffers more hostility. Eventually Paul goes alone to Athens in southern Greece while the rest of his team stays in the north.

Centuries before, Athens had been the intellectual capital of the world, where great philosophers like Socrates and Plato had framed some of the most important ideas of Western civilization. When Paul arrives, Athenians still see themselves as sophisticated intellectuals, but are really just into currently fashionable ideas. Despite the likelihood of rejection, Paul tries to engage them with the gospel.

8. In 17:16-34, where do you see Paul doing the following things?

Caring deeply for people, even though their culture is seriously misguided

Building bridges to connect with nonbelievers, rather than criticizing their flawed beliefs and practices

9. How would you describe your attitude toward nonbelievers around you, those you know personally and those in the culture at large?

- ☐ Frustrated. They don't listen, and I doubt they'll ever come to grips with their self-delusion.
- ☐ Angry. They're buying into God-substitutes and making a mess of the world with their immorality.

- ☐ Grieved. They need God, and underneath their bad behavior is emptiness that makes me deeply sad.
- ☐ Resigned. They don't want the gospel, and nothing I do is likely to change that.
- ☐ Respectful. They're wrong about a lot of things, but there's a lot of good in them, too.
- ☐ Grateful. Nonbelievers have been good friends to me, even though we disagree about some important things.
- ☐ Other (describe your thoughts and feelings):

10. How would you assess the results of Paul's outreach in Athens (17:32-34)? How successful was it? How worthwhile?

> One of the reasons we don't share the gospel more often is because we really don't care. So I think we need to start by saying, "Lord, You know my heart. Give me a heart for people who don't know You." (*Upside Down Living* 246–247)

11. To what extent do you invest time and energy relating with nonbelievers? A lot? A little? Not much? What motivates you to do that, or what gets in the way?

Notes and Observations

We can build bridges to nonbelievers by saying things like this:

> "You're a spiritual person? That's great, because I am, too. Since you care about spirituality, I'd really like to hear your view on the meaning of life. Would you share that with me?" Then *listen* to what they have to say.
> After you've heard them out, you might go on and say, "Tell me, according to your beliefs as a spiritual person, what do you think will happen to you after you die?" Again, listen carefully. And then say, "I'd like to give you my view."
> (*Upside Down Living* 251–252)

12. How could you build relationships with nonbelievers without adding more activities to your busy life? For instance, maybe there are nonbelievers among the parents who attend your children's sports practices. Maybe there are nonbelievers in your workplace.

13. After looking at Paul's example in these chapters, what is one thing you'd like to ask God for? Maybe it's the strength or faith to praise Him in a hard situation, or maybe it's deeper love for the nonbelievers around you. If you're meeting with a group, how can they pray for you?

SEVEN
MAKING EACH DAY COUNT
Acts 20:13–23:22

> To prepare for this discussion, please read:
> - Acts 20:13–23:22
> - Chapters 16 and 17 of *Upside Down Living*

In the film *The Bucket List*, two terminally ill men abandon their hospital to do the things they've always wanted to do before they "kick the bucket." They go skydiving, drag racing, and world traveling, and along the way they become true friends and learn how much it matters to love others and live as if each day matters.

What would you do with your time if you knew your days were numbered? When the apostle Paul left Greece and headed east to Jerusalem, the Holy Spirit repeatedly warned him that he would be arrested when he got there. He knew he faced a death sentence. His days were numbered, but he didn't go skydiving. Instead he pressed on, setting an example of how to live as if each day might be his last. In this session we'll look at five aspects of his example and focus on one key word: courage.

Notes and Observations

1. If you knew you had only one more year to live, how would you want to spend that time? (Don't feel obliged to come up with an impressive answer. Be honest. Is there something exciting and crazy you'd want to do? Something you'd want to write or make? People you'd want to talk to?)

In 20:17-35, Paul gives a farewell speech to the elders of the church in Ephesus. He is on his way to Jerusalem to take a financial gift from the Gentile churches he has planted to the Jewish Christians in Jerusalem, many of whom are poor. Paul hopes this act of generosity will strengthen the bonds of love between the Jewish and Gentile believers, but the Holy Spirit has warned him that Jerusalem isn't a safe place for him. In his speech to the elders, he asks them to follow his example in five ways:

- As a runner, competing to finish a race despite hindrances from the world, the flesh, and the Devil
- As a servant or steward, seeking to manage God's possessions in ways that further God's goals, not his own
- As a witness, describing what Jesus has done for him
- As a herald, speaking the message his King has given him
- As a watchman, looking out over the city walls and giving the bad or good news about what he sees

2. Paul wanted to "finish [his] race with joy" (20:24). What would finishing his race mean for Paul? What choices and habits would it involve?

3. What will finishing your race with joy involve for you?

Notes and Observations

Paul was focused on doing the "ministry" (20:24) or service God had assigned to him.

> A servant or slave owns very few possessions. And in the same way, I need to realize as God's servant that everything I have is on loan from Him. My life. My health. My career. My ministry. My possessions. My children. My future. It all belongs to God.
>
> So what's my objective as a steward of His possessions? To find out how God can bless *my* dreams and ambitions and goals? No, my objective is to discover His goals, His purposes, and align myself with these. It only makes sense; I'm His servant! . . .
>
> God wants to be in sole control of your life. He's the Master, I'm the servant. He's the Shepherd, I'm the sheep. He's the Potter, I'm the clay. I am the property of Jesus Christ, and I became that when I put my faith in Him. As Paul tells us in 1 Corinthians 6:20, "For you were bought at a price; therefore glorify God in your body and in your spirit, which are God's." (*Upside Down Living* 268–269)

4. What are some of God's goals for your life? What tasks has He given you?

Notes and Observations

5. How do those line up with, or conflict with, your own goals and dreams?

6. Do you think God cares about your dreams? When you think of a Master who tells you what to do and a Potter who shapes you, how do you connect that with someone who loves you?

Sure enough, Paul wasn't in Jerusalem long before he was arrested. A hearing in front of the Sanhedrin (Jewish high council) degenerated into chaos, and a plot to murder him was hatched. However, "The following night the Lord stood by him and said, 'Take courage, for as you have testified to the facts about me in Jerusalem, so you must testify also in Rome'" (Acts 23:11, ESV).

> Courage, also known as *bravery* or *fortitude*, is the ability to confront fear, pain, risk, danger, uncertainty or intimidation. Physical courage is bravery in the face of physical pain, hardship, or even the threat of death. . . .
> It was Mark Twain who said, "Courage is the mastery of fear. Not the absence of fear." . . . True courage is overcoming your fear in the face of adversity. As one person has said, "Courage is fear that has said its prayers." . . .
> There is moral courage, as well — courage to stand up for what's right. It takes courage to go against the whole current of our culture, and do the right thing today. It takes courage to follow the commands of Scripture, and to stand by what the Bible teaches. (*Upside Down Living* 279–280)

7. What reasons for courage did Paul have?

Notes and Observations

8. What reasons for courage do we have?

9. What do you think helps us build courage for facing hardship or standing up for what's right?

> Ultimately... you need to look to God for comfort. He will be with you, standing at your side, when all others have faded from the scene. (*Upside Down Living* 282)

10. How, in practical terms, do you go about looking to God for comfort and strength?

11. What if it feels like God is absent and we don't get the kind of clear words from the Lord that Paul got? Does that mean we're doing something wrong?

Notes and Observations

And when it's all said and done, what God wants from us is not success as much as faithfulness. Results and fruit are His responsibility. Faithfulness and obedience are ours.

Besides, what *is* success, anyway? Many of us tend to gauge success as "the bigger, the better." If it's big and popular, then it must be good.

But time has a way of sorting things out, doesn't it? What may be deemed a success today may be looked back on as a failure in the future. What may be looked upon today as a failure may be regarded as a success in days to come. You don't know until the dust settles, do you? And in that final day when we stand before Him, Jesus is *not* going to say, "Well done, good and *successful* servant." No, what He will say is, "Well done, good and faithful servant."

Faithfulness is what counts in God's kingdom. (*Upside Down Living* 285)

12. In what area of your life is the Lord asking you to be faithful — whether or not you're successful? How is that going?

13. If you're meeting with a group, pray for each person regarding the area he or she named in question 12. (You may want to divide into groups of two or three to do this.) Ask God to fill each person with His Spirit, strengthen your hearts with love and courage, and equip you to be persistent runners and faithful servants. Pray also for the nonbelievers on your list, asking God to give you a passionate heart like Paul's for those people.

If you're using this Bible study on your own, pray for yourself about these things. You can write your prayer here.

Notes and Observations

UPSIDE DOWN LIVING BIBLE STUDY

EIGHT
TRIALS AND STORMS
Acts 23:23–27:44

> To prepare for this discussion, please read:
> - Acts 23:23–27:44
> - Chapters 18 and 19 of *Upside Down Living*

Notes and Observations

The last chapters of Acts read like an adventure story. However, adventures of this kind are more fun to read than they are to live. Paul was tried multiple times before multiple judges and was moved from place to place to protect him from assassins. He languished in prison for years, at the whim of one governor after another, and was finally shipped to Rome for trial, but a storm tore apart his ship and the passengers barely survived. If this is the price we risk paying if we choose to be part of changing the world, then it's no wonder many people say no.

As you are reading this, Christians around the world are paying that price. They live in countries where it's dangerous, if not outright illegal, to be followers of Jesus. If you're blessed to live in a country where the danger isn't as severe as that, then thank God. Perhaps the faith and courage God asks of you are for other kinds of trial and shipwreck: the embarrassment of being ridiculed when you talk about Jesus; a financial storm; a terminal illness; the loss of a loved one. Often it's the ordinary Christian life well lived that changes one corner of the world. As we finish our study of Acts, ask the Holy Spirit to strengthen your soul through Paul's example.

Notes and Observations

1. Have you ever experienced a "shipwreck," a time when things went seriously wrong and significantly tested your faith and courage? If so, what was one really tough moment during that time?

Ironically, the people whose lives are sailing along on calm seas are often the most resistant to the gospel. Governor Felix, the judge in one of Paul's trials (24:1-23), was one such person.

> Felix had never seen anyone like Paul before. So confident. So sure. So bold, despite his circumstances. Intrigued, Felix, along with his wife Drusilla, spent private time with Paul.
>
> Drusilla happened to be Felix's third wife, and he had stolen her from another. Something in him wanted to know more about what this passionate Jew was saying, and Paul—never one to pull his punches—laid it out. The Bible tells us in Acts 24:25, "As he reasoned with them about righteousness and self-control and the judgment to come, Felix was terrified. 'Go away for now,' he replied. 'When it is more convenient, I'll call for you again.'"
>
> I think Felix had really wanted to know more, but when Paul got down to the brass tacks, it made the loose-living governor very, very uncomfortable; talking about morality and integrity—not to mention God's judgment—weren't topics he was used to dealing with. So Felix said, "Okay. Stop. Time out. I think that's enough for now." (*Upside Down Living* 295)

Notes and Observations

2. What might Paul have said to Felix about the following topics? What does the gospel say about them? (The passages suggested below may help you.)

   Righteousness (Romans 1:16-20)

   Self-control (Romans 1:21-32)

   The judgment to come (Romans 2:12-16; Matthew 25:31-46)

3. Why are people like Felix often so uncomfortable with those topics?

4. Can we talk about the gospel of Christ without getting into those subjects? Explain.

Notes and Observations

5. In Acts 26:1-23, Paul tells King Agrippa the story of his conversion. Why does he do this? Is this an attempt to get himself released from prison?

> You can believe that Jesus Christ is the Son of God and the Bible to be the Word of God, and still not be a Christian. Listen to what James says about the "faith" of demons: "You believe that there is one God. You do well. Even the demons believe—and tremble!" (James 2:19). . . .
>
> Mere intellectual assent to certain truths isn't all there is. Saving faith has to go beyond that.
>
> The fact is, you can read the Bible, pray, keep the Ten Commandments to the best of your ability, attend church on a regular basis, and even be baptized, yet still not necessarily be a Christian.
>
> I'll take it a step even further. You can make some visible changes in your life that would *look like* conversion to some, and not necessarily be a Christian. . . .
>
> "All right, then," someone might reply, "what exactly *do* you need to do to be a Christian?" The answer comes from the Lord Himself, as quoted by the apostle. Here was Paul's calling in a nutshell: "*To open their eyes, so they may turn from darkness to light and from the power of Satan to God. Then they will receive forgiveness for their sins and be given a place among God's people, who are set apart by faith in Me*" [Acts 26:18].
>
> This is the essential gospel message—what needs to happen for a person to come to faith.
>
> *First, your eyes must be opened.* . . .
>
> *Second, you have to turn from darkness to light.*
>
> Here's how it works: Only God can open your eyes; only you can turn from darkness to light. Only God can make

you aware of your need for Christ; only you can put your faith in Christ. God won't do it for you. He has given you a free will, and it's up to you to respond and decide. (*Upside Down Living* 294, 300–301)

6. Read 26:18. What does it mean to have your eyes opened? How is that different from intellectually believing the right information about Jesus?

What is God's role in having your eyes opened?

7. What does it mean to turn from darkness to light? How is that different from simply behaving as properly as you can?

Christianity is not a buffet. It's not a salad bar, where you pick this or that ingredient and leave out the things that don't appeal to you. *"Let's see. . . . I'll have a helping of forgiveness and a little side of mercy. And I'm going to pass on the conviction and the guilt. I'm on a guilt-free diet, you know!"* (*Upside Down Living* 292–293)

Notes and Observations

Notes and Observations

8. If someone realizes that despite being a churchgoer and trying to live a good life, he or she hasn't turned from darkness to light, what should that person do?

After Paul spoke to Agrippa, he was sent by ship to Rome for a trial. But a terrible storm arose at sea, and after many days without food, when the crew was in despair, Paul told them, "For there stood by me this night an angel of the God to whom I belong and whom I serve, saying, 'Do not be afraid, Paul; you must be brought before Caesar; and indeed God has granted you all those who sail with you.' Therefore take heart, men, for I believe God that it will be just as it was told me" (27:23-25).

9. What does it mean to say we belong to God? What are the implications of that?

Sometimes we will come to God and say, "What's going on with these events in my life? What's all this about?" And God may reply, "You don't need to know right now. But in time, I will make it known to you."

The Bible says in Romans 8:28, "We know that all things work together for good to those that love God and are called according to His purpose." It doesn't say we will *see* all things work together. . . . Because we can't always see (or even imagine) how certain things could result in good for anybody. But we can *know* that they will — by faith — and that God will give us more details when He is ready. Until that time, we must trust. (*Upside Down Living* 284)

TRIALS AND STORMS **69**

10. Paul trusted God's promise to get him to Rome and ultimately to God Himself after death. What promises has God made to you?

Notes and Observations

11. What do faithfulness and trust involve for you in your current situation? How is that going?

12. As you look back over the whole of this study, what are the key things you will take away from it?

13. This session raises sensitive issues, so if you're meeting with a group, be sure to pray for one another.

- Pray for those who are in the midst of storms. Ask God to let them know He is with them and will carry them through to the other side. Ask God if you can be of any practical help.
- Pray for those who need confidence that they belong to God.
- Pray for those who have realized they have been almost Christians and want to be real Christians. Give them a chance to voice their decision to turn from darkness to light, and ask God to help them sustain that commitment.

Notes and Observations

- Pray for nonbelievers in your lives who may be reluctant to deal with the truth about righteousness, self-control, and judgment. Ask God to show you how you can help them.
- Thank God for what He has done for each of you as you've studied the book of Acts. Ask Him to show you what He has in store for you as you move forward.

LEADER'S NOTES

If this is your first time leading a small-group discussion, don't worry. You don't need to know the perfect answers to the questions, and you don't need to be an expert in the book of Acts. What you do need is a willingness to read portions of Acts and *Upside Down Living* each week, think about the questions ahead of time and read these Leader's Notes, and ask the Holy Spirit to work in your life and the lives of your group members.

Leader's Job Description

Your role is to:

- *Help people bond as a group*, especially if they don't know each other well. The first question in each session invites people to say a little about themselves as they start thinking about the topic at hand. If people are shy at first, you can go first on question 1. (Normally you should *not* go first in answering the questions.) Give a genuine answer, and keep it under one minute long. Ask everyone else to keep their answers to a minute, rather than telling long stories, so that this question doesn't consume all your time. The intent is to break the ice and get to know things about each other that don't usually come out in small talk.
- *Keep the discussion moving.* Encourage people to have a conversation rather than just going around the circle and sharing answers to each question. You can ask follow-up questions like, "Why do you think that's the case?" "Can you say more about that?" "What do others think?" "Is there a particular place in Acts that

supports that idea?" "Does the book shed any light on this?"

- *Keep the group on track* when they're tempted to go off on a tangent. If people get bogged down on a question or go off topic, you can say, "I'm going to interrupt here and bring us back to the text." "Does anyone else have thoughts on question 2?" "Let's go on to the next question. Could someone read it aloud?"
- *Make sure that everyone gets a chance to talk* and no one dominates. It's not necessary that every person respond aloud to every question, but every person should have the chance. Sometimes it's necessary to interrupt a talkative person and say, "Thanks, Joe. What do others think?" You, too, should not dominate the discussion. See more below under "Guiding the Discussion."
- *Make sure the discussion remains respectful.* See the ground rules below.
- *Pray for your group.* Ask the Holy Spirit to fill each person, increase their faith and courage, and empower them to share the gospel with those around them. Many of them may never have led someone to Christ. Ask God to do more through them than they can imagine.

Preparing for the Discussion

You'll probably want to read the chapters from *Upside Down Living* before each group meeting. If you can, work through your own responses to the discussion questions ahead of time. Even though you won't be sharing your answers each time, thinking through the questions will help you form follow-up questions.

Guiding the Discussion

A few ground rules can make people comfortable discussing what they really think:

- *Confidentiality:* Whatever is said in the group stays in the group. Nothing is to be repeated to those who weren't there.
- *Honesty:* We're not here to impress each other. We're here to grow and to know each other.
- *Respect:* Disagreement is welcome. Disrespect is not.

Ask for a volunteer to read each question aloud before you discuss it. In some cases it will also be helpful for someone to read aloud the text between the questions.

Encourage people to talk to each other rather than just to you. When someone shares an answer, avoid replying with your own views. Instead, ask what others think. If someone says something seriously unbiblical, give others in the group a chance to say what is true rather than doing it yourself. If no one does, say something like, "There's a Bible passage that sheds light on what we're discussing. Can someone find Ephesians XX:XX and read it aloud?" Do your best to let the group arrive at what the Bible teaches, and take on the role of teacher only as a last resort.

Likewise, avoid the temptation to answer a question if others are silent. Don't be afraid of silence. Wait for the group. People often need time to think. If you answer the questions, people will learn to wait for you, and discussion will be squelched. Sometimes it's helpful to rephrase the question in your own words. Then wait for others' responses.

It's not necessary to read aloud the entire portion of Acts for each group discussion. However, the notes below suggest some passages you may want to read aloud. You can omit some passages if your time is limited. You can have one reader for a passage, or if you're more adventurous you can assign roles to various readers. The notes list the roles for each reading. Have people skip phrases like "he said" and "they answered."

Notes and Observations

Session 1: Power to Change the World

Reading

If you'd like to read Acts 1:1-11 aloud like a play, you'll need volunteers to read these roles:

- Narrator
- Jesus
- Two men dressed in white (angels)

For 2:1-41 you'll need:

- Narrator
- The crowd (could be one person or several)
- Peter
- The prophet Joel (his prophecy comes in the middle of Peter's speech)
- King David (lines from his psalms come in the middle of Peter's speech)

You can skip phrases like "they said" and "he said to them."

Discussion

Questions 1–2. Each discussion begins with an approach question which invites group members to share something about themselves relating to the topic at hand. This discussion begins with two such questions. With these questions it's appropriate to go around the circle and give everyone a chance to respond. (With later questions, though, going around the circle will hinder free-flowing discussion and lead to boredom.) Also, with these questions it's appropriate for you to answer. (With other questions, most of the time you should refrain from answering so that you don't stifle discussion by pronouncing the "right" answer.)

Question 4. The disciples will testify to what they have seen and heard of Jesus (their own experiences). They will also testify to what He has taught them and to what they have learned from the Scriptures about the meaning of His life, death, and resurrection. Peter's sermon in Acts 2 shows all of these aspects of being a witness.

Question 5. We can speak with people one-on-one about our own experience of Jesus and about what we've learned from the Bible about His message and work. We can also demonstrate the truth of His teachings by doing the things He said to do, such as loving our enemies and caring for those in need.

Question 6. You may want to walk the group through the definition. Some in the group may not have experienced thinking Christ's thoughts. You could ask someone to describe a hypothetical situation and then discuss what it would be like to think Christ's thoughts in that situation, as well as how that might affect a person's actions.

Question 8. If people are shy about admitting the challenges of a busy life, you can set the tone by being honest about the challenges you face. How do you carve out time to spend time with God (if you do)? What trade-offs do you have to make? This question offers a chance to be honest with each other and agree to support each other in the costly decision to make time for God's Word, so that we can be filled with His Spirit and do His work in the world.

Question 9. For instance, we might say faith is not simply agreeing with a list of facts about Christ. It is that plus trust in Christ, a surrender of one's life to Him based on that trust, and the behavior that flows naturally from that surrender. You can explain trust by comparing it to trust in a spouse. Surrender is somewhat like acknowledging the authority of a commanding officer in the military, and somewhat like surrender to intimacy with a lover.

Sin is a refusal to trust and surrender, an insistence on one's own way. It's like breaking one's marriage vows or, in another way, like disobeying orders from a commanding officer. (These aren't the only possible analogies — you may have better ones.)

Notes and Observations

To repent is to change one's thinking, like making a U-turn and changing the direction in which one is driving.

Question 10. Only God can overcome the current sense that sin is an outmoded notion. Our part is to explain it accurately and winsomely (finger-wagging is often counterproductive), to pray, and to set an example of what a life of rejecting sin can look like.

Question 11. A few possible questions: What do you do on a typical Wednesday morning? What are the big issues you're dealing with in your life right now? What do you believe is truly important in life? Do you believe there is a God? If so, what do you think God is like? If not, what do you believe ultimate reality is like? (For instance, is the material world all that exists?)

Session 2: Secrets of the Early Church

Reading
To read 2:42–4:31 aloud as a play, you'll need these roles:

- Narrator
- Peter (and John)
- Annas the high priest, other priests, and the Sanhedrin (this can be one reader)
- The believers praying (this can be one reader)

You can skip phrases like "he said" and "they answered."

Discussion
Question 2. Some of us don't want to believe this, because we are preoccupied with other concerns and don't want to feel guilty that we're not participating more with what God is doing. Some of us compare ourselves to other people, especially celebrities or prominent people in our own church, and therefore feel we have no significant gifts to offer. Group members can help each other perceive what they could contribute.

Question 3. It's important to be honest here. If your group finds this difficult, set an example by honestly sharing your priorities and challenges. All of us have weaknesses, and you don't have to impress your group by appearing perfect. You might ask each person, "If you could grow more faithful in one of these areas in the next year, which would it be?" Talk about things that get in the way, like busyness or the tendency for the mind to wander during prayer.

Question 4. Peter and John show fear of God by obeying Him despite the temple leadership's reaction which led to painful consequences. Peter and John feared God more than other people and more than physical pain. Likewise, the community focused its prayer on God's greatness and power which dwarfed the power of humans who opposed the gospel. The more we fear God, the less we fear other things and people.

Notes and Observations

In fact, if you want to know what someone's true "god" is, look at what they most fear.

Question 5. Ironically, a healthy fear of God draws us to respect and even trust Him more, because we know He's powerful and we fear other things less. Reading Scripture passages that display His greatness can feed a healthy fear. Look at some of the many passages where people encounter angels or the Lord and they are so overcome that the angel has to tell them, "Fear not!" or "Don't be afraid!" Isaiah 6, Luke 1, and Revelation 1 are good places to start.

Question 7. The Psalms are full of prayers in which the psalmist is utterly honest about his anguish and yet praises God. He doesn't cover up the anguish; he offers it to God along with his praise. Look at Psalm 22, for example. Psalm 88 is even darker, and yet throughout it, the psalmist is looking to God, not to false comforts that might numb his pain.

Question 8. Possibilities include fear of God (and confidence in God), boldness, close relationships with one another, and generosity with the needy.

Session 3: A Person God Uses

Reading
Read Acts 4:32–5:11 aloud. You'll need these roles:

- Narrator
- Peter
- Sapphira

Read 6:1–7:60 aloud. (If that's too much, you can do 6:1-15 and 7:51-60.) You'll need:

- Narrator
- The Twelve (the apostles)
- False witnesses (6:11,13-14)
- Stephen

Discussion
This session covers three portions of Acts: the story of Ananias and Sapphira's hypocrisy, the story of Stephen's courage and murder, and the story of Philip's evangelism. The liars and truth-tellers offer a stark contrast to each other. If your time is limited and you find you're getting a lot out of the earlier questions, you may choose to skip the discussion of Philip.

Question 1. Some of us feel pressure to put up an appearance at work, or with our families, or (unfortunately) at church. You don't need to spend a lot of time with this question — the point is to help group members think of situations in which they're tempted to fake it.

Question 2. They wanted people to think they were more generous and less attached to their possessions than they really were.

Question 3. Ananias and Sapphira weren't faking it in front of people and then going to God privately and being honest about their attachment to their stuff. Hypocrites rarely have honest prayer lives — faking it becomes a habit. And

Notes and Observations

because the people of God are a temple of the Holy Spirit (1 Corinthians 3:16; Ephesians 2:19-22), lying to the people of God is equivalent to lying to the Holy Spirit.

Questions 4–5. Praising God when we don't feel like it is acting in honest accord with our deepest beliefs, as opposed to being controlled by our feelings. Feelings go up and down, so acting according to our feelings isn't integrity and authenticity; it's just moodiness, impulsiveness. On the other hand, a person who doesn't acknowledge Jesus as Savior and Lord would be hypocritical if she sang worship songs to Him. She could participate in a concert performance, but it would be a performance, not worship. Likewise, to sing worship songs while one has an ongoing habit of persistent sin is also hypocritical, because to truly call Jesus Lord involves doing what He says to do.

Question 6. Stephen takes on a task that involves practical care for those in need. He yields himself so fully to the Holy Spirit that the Spirit is free to do powerful works through him. Stephen talks about Jesus with his fellow Jews, even though he knows this could be dangerous, because drawing others to God is more important than his safety. He plays out this commitment to the very end by speaking boldly for Christ, and then forgives those who oppose him.

Question 7. "Full of the Holy Spirit" means permeated by the Holy Spirit so that He guides all that we think and do. Wisdom is knowing how to put the principles of the Scriptures into practice in daily life. It is perceiving the godly thing to do in a specific situation. Faithfulness is following through and doing that godly thing, even when it's uncomfortable or costly.

Question 8. In the Bible, angels aren't cuddly babies with sweet smiles. They are radiant with holiness, and they often terrify people who see them. Their goodness is powerful and inspires awe. See for example Revelation 10:1-3; 22:8-9.

Question 11. It's natural to be angry and defensive when we or other Christians are attacked. To develop a habit of turning those feelings over to God rather than striking back is a process that involves prayer, meditation on the example of Jesus and others like Stephen in Scripture, honesty with ourselves and those we trust, and other habits of spiritual growth.

Questions 12–14. Some Christians have very little contact with people who are different from them. A first step is simply being aware of that fact, and then looking around our lives for those who are different, people we may be holding at arm's length without realizing it.

Question 15. Is your group a safe place for people to come clean? As leader, do you set an example of being honest with the group about what you're giving God and what your limitations are, or do you feel like you have to appear to have it all together because you're the leader? The group doesn't need you to seem like Stephen if you're not. They need you to be real and in the process of seeking to give God more of yourself.

Session 4: The Last Person You'd Expect

Reading
Read Acts 7:58–8:3 aloud. You'll need:

- Narrator
- Stephen

Read 9:1-30 aloud. You'll need:

- Narrator
- Jesus
- Saul
- Ananias
- The people who heard Saul (9:21)

Discussion
Question 2. Initially, Stephen's death seems to Saul like exactly the right thing, and Saul sets out to bring down the rest of those who share Stephen's beliefs. Saul thinks the followers of Jesus are blaspheming God and distorting the true Jewish way of life. His methods are drastic and violent, but his hatred of what he thinks is blasphemy and heresy shows a man zealous for God (as he understands God) and for what he thinks is truth, bold, self-confident, willing to throw himself into the cause. Once Jesus knocks him down and shows him that Stephen was right, all those qualities that made him a zealous enemy will help him as a zealous apostle.

Question 3. The people of God are the body of Christ on earth, the temple of the Holy Spirit. What is done to the people of God is done to Christ Himself (Matthew 25:40,45).

Question 4. God is infinitely merciful. His kingdom isn't just for the people who have been good all their lives. He specializes in welcoming those who have been His enemies.

Questions 5–6. Ananias understandably didn't want to go to Saul and admit to being a follower of Jesus, because the Saul he'd heard of would arrest him and have him killed. It took enormous faith and courage for Ananias to believe what the Lord was telling him in prayer, despite Saul's reputation.

Question 7. The risks of saying no are often hard to guess. What if Stephen had said no? What if Ananias had said no? Would Saul — the man who wrote much of the New Testament — not have been converted? Our disobedience may cost us, but it may cost others even more.

Question 8. Unlike Ananias and Sapphira, Barnabas actually did sell significant property and give the money for the care of the needy in the church. Later, he saw evidence that Saul's conversion was genuine and put his own reputation on the line to vouch for Saul when church leaders doubted him. He gained a reputation for discernment, became a leader in the church, and was even sent as an emissary to assess the radical ministry to the Gentiles in Antioch. He found that the ministry there was in accord with what the apostles taught, so he moved from Jerusalem to Antioch to help out. He also perceived Saul's gifts and recruited Saul to work with him. He was generous, farsighted, a strategic thinker, and a person who cared about individuals.

Question 10. It's easy to get so busy that we don't notice or don't have time for those who are younger in faith. We may get so busy trying to be leaders or laborers that we forget to be a Barnabas and take the time to mentor someone. We don't have to be a lot further along the road than someone else. We just need to make ourselves available. But the pressures of life are real. Busyness is a theme of this study because it is an obstacle that most of us have to contend with if we want to live like the people of Acts.

Session 5: Beyond the Comfort Zone

Reading
Read Acts 10:1-48 aloud. You'll need:

- Narrator
- Cornelius
- The Lord (10:13,15) and the Spirit (10:19-20)
- Peter
- Men (10:22)

Discussion
Question 2. The voice is saying that if God is changing the rules from what they were under the Old Covenant, then His followers have no business clinging to the old rules. If God says a food is now clean to eat — or if He says a group of people are now welcome into the covenant community — then that's how it is. The Gentiles, who were unclean, can now be made clean by faith in Christ.

Reading
Read 12:1-19 aloud. You'll need:

- Narrator
- Angel
- Peter
- Servant girl
- Believers (12:15)

Discussion
Question 4. Establish a group atmosphere where it's safe for people to say what they don't understand about God. Don't be too quick to defend God. Yes, God is sovereign and good, so He always has a good reason for doing what He does. But He often doesn't tell us those reasons, and voicing our hurt and confusion can be a significant part of our spiritual growth.

While it's important to affirm what we know about God, it's also important to face what we don't know.

Question 5. After telling the truth about our confusion, we can strengthen our trust by thinking about God's long track record of goodness toward us personally and humankind generally. We can look at His decision to give us life in the first place (He didn't have to) and His centuries-long labor to redeem us from our bad choices, a labor that culminated in the life, death, and resurrection of Christ. The cross is our number one reason to trust Him.

Reading

Read 14:8–14:28 aloud. You'll need:

- Narrator
- Paul (and Barnabas)
- The crowd

Discussion

Question 8. Paul shows enormous courage and fortitude (sticking to right action even when it's really hard). He's absolutely committed to communicating the gospel and to the people in the churches he's established. He's practical about organizing those churches so they can sustain themselves.

Questions 9–10. Invite group members to talk about what they would do in current situations if they had a lot of fortitude (for instance). Courage, fortitude, and passion for the gospel aren't qualities one can just decide to have more of. They are the kind of qualities one develops over time. Consistent prayer and internalizing the Word of God helps. Asking for the Holy Spirit's help and then taking a step of fortitude — and doing that over and over again — helps. Admitting one's weakness helps. Getting encouragement and prayer from other believers helps.

Session 6: Songs in the Dark

Reading
Read Acts 16:6-40. You'll need:

- Narrator
- A man of Macedonia
- Lydia
- Slave girl
- Paul (and Silas)
- Slave girl's owners (16:20–21)
- Jailer
- Magistrates (16:35)

Discussion
Question 1. You don't need to belabor this question. Its purpose is to help people know one another and themselves. Answers depend on a person's temperament and circumstances, not just spiritual maturity. Some people are wired with more natural optimism. For a person who is naturally melancholy or is in a hard place, significant growth in Christ may mean being a 3 when they'd normally be a 1.

Question 3. They deal with obstacles to their plans, harassment from an evil spirit, rage from the slave girl's owners, insults, an ugly trial, beating, prison, and the stocks.

Question 4. They believe serious suffering is a normal part of the Christian life (14:22). They are convinced that God is good and in charge no matter how painful their circumstances are. They believe their situation is a chance to give glory to God by showing others how Christians deal with suffering. They believe it's more important to draw others to Christ than to have a comfortable life.

Question 6. Encourage honesty here. Many of us aren't willing to go as far as Paul. But could we go a bit farther than we are now? Maybe we won't choose situations where we might be beaten and jailed, but what about enduring ridicule?

Reading

Read 17:16-34. You'll need:

- Narrator
- Men of Athens (17:19,32)
- Paul

Discussion

Question 8. Paul's distress over idolatry (verse 16) didn't make him want to distance himself from the Athenians. It made him want to move toward them, even at risk of rejection, because he cared about them. In 17:22–28 he goes out of his way to affirm the Athenians' interest in religion, the teaching of their poets, and their intelligence.

Question 10. Most rejected Paul, but a few believed. Each person is valuable.

Question 11. Guilt is not the point here. Help your group talk honestly and not defensively about their motivations and priorities. People are busy. They like to be with people who are like them, not people who see the world very differently. If all you achieve is getting people to take a good look at their lives, that may be progress.

Question 12. Again, small steps are okay.

Session 7: Making Each Day Count

Reading
Read Acts 20:17-38. You'll need:

- Narrator
- Paul

Discussion

Question 2. Finishing his race would include continuing to proclaim the gospel of God's grace to the end of his life despite violent opposition. It would involve prison and hardship (20:23) as well as uncertainty. It would require, for example, the choice to trust God, habits of prayer and obedience and unselfishness, and refusal to give in to despair.

Question 3. Answers may include, for instance, trust in God, habits of prayer and obedience, courage, and the refusal to be distracted by despair, pleasure-seeking, comfort-seeking, ego, or fear of rejection.

Questions 4–5. He has given each of us a sphere of influence where He asks us to serve Him by being good friends, good neighbors, loving members of families, honorable workers. He may ask us to make things that are beautiful or useful. He may ask us to speak or write what is true. He asks us to worship Him, build up the community of believers, and reach out to those in need physically and/or spiritually. He gives us tasks that fit the way we are uniquely made, so often our dreams fit with His. But sometimes they don't. Saul had to change his goals after he encountered Jesus. Sometimes our goals (for example, fame and fortune) don't interest God. When that happens, the story of Abraham's sacrifice (Genesis 22) is a good one to meditate on.

Question 6. It's enormously important to become convinced, deep in our gut, that the Master both cares deeply about our dreams and has the right to say no to them. Many of us think authority figures are inherently selfish and uncaring, and we need to bring those thoughts to light and examine them honestly. Rather than pushing people to give the right answer here, help them come clean about the nagging doubts that keep them from fully trusting God. Help them come clean about the distorted notion that love equals letting us be in charge.

Reading

Read Acts 22:30–23:22. You'll need:

- Narrator
- Paul
- Others at the trial (23:4,9)
- The Lord (23:11)
- Plotters (23:14-15)
- Centurion (23:18)
- Commander (23:19,22)
- Paul's nephew (23:20-21)

Discussion

Questions 7–8. We, like Paul, can take courage from the fact that God will not allow anything to *ultimately* harm us. God may let us suffer physically or emotionally in this life, but the core of who we are is completely safe, and we will live eternally with Him. He will also bring good out of our suffering, even if we can't see that good here and now.

Questions 9–10. You talked about this in session 5, and you can go deeper now. Exactly how does God's Word help us build courage? Share some ways of internalizing Scripture and how that gets at the roots of fear. How does time alone with God and ourselves help us? How can a group like this one help? How does worship help? What does the Holy Spirit do, and how do we cooperate with His work?

Question 11. Feelings aren't good guides as to whether God is present. Sometimes He lets us feel His presence, and sometimes He lets us feel His absence so that our trust will

Notes and Observations

grow deeper. It's helpful to have one or more spiritual friends to check in with to make sure we're not off course through sin or misunderstanding. But God's silence doesn't automatically mean we're off course.

Session 8: Trials and Storms

Reading
Have someone read Acts 24:24-27.
Read 25:23–26:32 as a play. You'll need:

- Narrator
- Festus
- Herod Agrippa
- Paul

Read 27:13-26. You'll need:

- Narrator
- Paul

Discussion
Question 1. There isn't time for people to tell their whole story at the beginning of your meeting, so ask them to share one tough moment now, and you can hear the rest of the story later.

Question 2. Even a non-Jew like Felix knows it is important to be a righteous (just, virtuous) person. Paul asserts that the Creator God is the judge in such matters and that a right relationship with Him is what counts as righteousness. Felix has no relationship with this God, and his behavior is unrighteous even by Roman standards. He lacks self-control, the ability to govern his desires and impulses so that he behaves with integrity. He is Paul's judge on earth, but the Creator will judge all people by their actions, and by that standard Felix will be condemned to a harsh fate.

Question 3. Immoral people obviously don't like to have their immorality pointed out. But beyond that, powerful people like Felix don't like to be told that there is someone more powerful than they, to whom they will have to give account. They like to think they're in charge of their lives and can do what they want. They hate to be told that they're not

Notes and Observations

even in control of their own behavior because they're slaves to their impulses.

Question 4. The gospel isn't the gospel without this "bad news." See *Upside Down Living* 43–47.

Question 5. Astonishingly, Paul is focused on what Agrippa needs (Christ), even at the risk of his own future. Ask the group what they think it takes to be that oriented toward others' needs.

Question 6. Our eyes are opened when God enables us to overcome Satan's blinding so we are convinced at our core that we need a Savior, and that Jesus is that Savior who deserves our wholehearted allegiance. It's not just the mind saying, "Okay, I get it." It's the Spirit saying, "Yes, I embrace this!" Only God can open someone's eyes (2 Corinthians 4:3-4; Ephesians 1:18).

Question 7. To turn from darkness to light is to surrender to Christ as both Savior and Master, and to choose the behavior that corresponds to that surrender. God doesn't do this for us; we have to surrender. It's not just proper behavior; it's surrendered behavior (Romans 13:11-14).

Question 8. It's possible that you may have someone in your group who is ready to take this step of surrender. They may or may not want to do it in front of everyone. Talk about the kinds of things a person should say to God at this point: "Yes, Lord, I believe that You are the Son of God who died for me. I surrender to You. I ask Your forgiveness for my rebellion. I gratefully accept Your forgiveness, and I want to live Your way. Please fill me with Your Spirit." Invite anyone to take this step either now, later with you alone, or on their own.

Question 9. It means we're part of His family, and nothing can separate us from His love (Romans 8:31-39). It also means we're His servants and have agreed to do what He says. We're no longer slaves to our own compulsions but are voluntary servants of God (Romans 6:15-23).

Question 10. See how many you can name. Just in Romans 8 you can find at least a dozen.

Don't leave the world the same way you found it.

Upside Down Living
Greg Laurie

In this exciting overview of the book of Acts, Greg Laurie reminds us that our mission as believers has never changed. Today, just as it was two thousand years ago, those who belong to Christ need to make a seismic impact on their culture.

978-0-98018-317-7

To order copies, call NavPress at **1-800-366-7788** or log on to **www.NavPress.com**.

NAVPRESS
Discipleship Inside Out®

Other Books by Greg Laurie

As I See It
Better Than Happiness
Daily Hope for Hurting Hearts
Dealing with Giants
Deepening Your Faith
Discipleship
Essentials
For Every Season, volumes 1, 2, and 3
God's Design for Christian Dating
The Great Compromise
The Greatest Stories Ever Told, volumes 1, 2, and 3
His Christmas Presence
Hope
Hope for America
Hope for Hurting Hearts
How to Know God
I'm Going on a Diet Tomorrow
Living Out Your Faith
Making God Known
Married. Happily.
Run to Win
Secrets to Spiritual Success
Signs of the Times
Start! To Follow
Strengthening Your Faith
Ten Things You Should Know About God and Life
Upside Down Living
What Every Christian Needs to Know
Why, God?
Worldview

Visit www.AllenDavidBooks.com

KERYGMA PUBLISHING